Palaver Finish

Palaver Finish

Essays by Chenjerai Hove

WEAVER
PRESS

Weaver Press, Box A1922, Avondale, Harare, Zimbabwe

Published in South Africa by M & G Books, Johannesburg
7 Quince Road, Milpark, 2092, www.mg.co.za

Earlier versions of these articles have appeared in
The Zimbabwe Standard newspaper, and are used with permission.

Typeset by Fontline Electronic Publishing, Harare, Zimbabwe.
Cover designed by Inkspots, Harare

ISBN: 1 77922 001 4

✿ Contents ✿

✿   ✿

Chris Pennarts

Chenjerai Hove was born in Mazvihwa communal area, southern Zimbabwe, near the mining town of Zvishavane. Novelist, poet, essayist and lecturer, his published works include *Masimba Avanhu?*(1986), *Bones* (winner of the Zimbabwe literary prize in 1988, and the 1989 Noma Award for publishing in Africa), *Shadows*, (1991), *Ancestors* (1994), *Shebeen Tales* (essays, 1994), *Up in Arms* (1982), *Swimming in Floods of Tears* (with Lyamba wa Kabika, 1983), *Red Hills of Home* (1985), *Rainbows in the Dust* (1997), *Guardians of the Soil* (with Iliya Trojanow, 1997).

He has travelled extensively throughout Africa, Europe and the United States on lecture tours, and has acted as writer-in-residence at the universities of Zimbabwe, Leeds, Lewis and Clark (Oregon) and Leiden.

Hove's books have been translated into several languages, including French, German, Japanese, Norwegian, Swedish, Dutch and Danish.

ஃ Africa's Abused Soldiers ஃ

You are a Karanga gentleman drinking your last cent in a bar in Masvingo. It had to be the last one since you have this other friend, a Zezuru whom you went to school with and he has come to see you all the way from Harare. It is only polite that you tell his purse to take a rest while you take care of all the financial proceedings. But then there is this Ndebele friend whom the Zezuru friend still remembers from those old school days.

'Yes, he is also working here. I phoned to say you were coming,' you say. The Zezuru friend is excited. Soon, the Ndebele friend arrives, hand in hand with your other friend, the Ndau gentleman you also went to school with. There is time to make merry. Four friends from all the corners of the country. All the money becomes everyone's money. You drink and talk about how life has been all these years. One of you has a broken leg sustained in an accident. The other has a scar on the face from some political violence of one form or another.

Suddenly, the windows of the bar are bashed in and there is broken glass all over the place. Several young soldiers with hot blood in their veins arrive and take over the bar. They beat all of you up, with sticks and knobkerries, crushing everything in their way. You only watch as they beat you and your helpless friends, and everyone else in the pub.

The young soldiers break into the till at the counter and take all the evening's earnings with them. They even ask everybody to put all their money on the table. You and your friends do as instructed. As the soldiers walk away, you soon hear that they have done that to the other nightclubs and pubs in Zimbabwe's oldest town.

'But we are peaceful guys. Why did they do that? We did not even vote for the opposition during the last mayoral elections,' your Ndebele friend whispers, just in case the uniformed men of violence come back to interrupt the discussion with more broken glass and blows to the innocent human body.

'They beat me recently, in Epworth. You know that is where I stay these days. They just came into the bar where I was drinking and beat up everyone in there. They even killed a few people. I was lucky to survive. That is why I thought I could escape for a while and take the journey to Masvingo to see my friends. They raid every day, armed with guns and sticks, beating up everyone, asking them why they voted for the opposition,' the Zezuru gentleman informs the others.

'But with all those balancing rocks around, Epworth is a good place for balance,' the Ndebele man becomes poetic. The men talk about balance and imbalance. I can hear them still, in my imagination, as they discuss the abused soldiers of the African continent.

Recently in Zambia, a female opposition politician, a former minister at that, was invaded by a whole truckload of heavily armed policemen and soldiers, wielding loaded AK47s. When she took refuge in another family's house, the whole family was arrested at gunpoint. Fortunately, she had gone out through the back door, into the nearby bush. On realising that they had just missed her by a whisker, the soldiers surrounded the bush in which they suspected the woman was hiding. They set fire to the grass. Luckily, she managed to give them the slip.

The story is the same all over the African continent. The soldiers are treated like a political militia, saluting the President of the Republic by name, not by position. They begin to belong personally to the Head of State, not to the state.

As institutions of violence, African armies are used to torture political opponents instead of defending the citizenry in case of external attack. Shamelessly, our army generals agree to take such orders as shooting at people protesting over food prices. The generals even hold rallies during which they instruct their juniors to vote for the politician of the ruling party.

All the disappearances, torture and cruelty in African countries are inflicted on people by the very soldiers who are supposed to defend them. They throw people to the crocodiles, or take them up into the air by helicopter and drop them into the rivers of Africa.

The army and presidential militias are responsible for mass graves all over the continent, killing people, shooting political opponents of the republic's leaders in the vain conviction that they are serving the nation. They are no longer the people's army. They are, indeed, the people's enemies.

Gruesome murders and torture, the army is in charge.

In Zimbabwe, the soldiers are now pegging illegally acquired farms. Everyone knows that they have no knowledge of surveying and agricultural planning. And yet the politicians openly send them to participate in committing a crime.

Even when they are asked to kill the political opponents of the rulers, the soldiers know only too well that they are committing a crime. Crime after crime after crime.

I know that political scientists have studied why there are coups in Africa. For me it is simple: after being ordered to participate in crime, the soldiers no longer have any respect for the political leaders. So, one day they get fed up with committing other people's crimes. They turn the gun to state house and shoot to kill. Their consciences reach bursting point. They become tired of wearing other people's dirty underpants.

In this century, it is important for our army commanders to simply stand up to the politicians and tell them that they cannot obey criminal orders. The police, secret service and all the other secret this or that must refuse to haunt innocent people who are proclaimed the enemies of the republic by those who think they are the super-patriots. Everyone who does not think like them is declared an enemy, and so must be shot in the public square. Students are shot in the streets. Workers are haunted by an army platoon sent to quell a potential work stoppage. Airports teem with armed men and women. Broadcasting stations are manned by armed men ordered to shoot to kill.

On Armed Forces Day, our soldiers are made to display dilapidated armoured cars and tanks that any modern army can destroy in a few seconds. All in the pursuit of military might and force against internal political opponents.

The army becomes personalised. The soldiers owe their allegiance to a single man. And that man begins to think the post of President is a personal matter, some kind of monarchy after an election. The post of President or Prime Minister is not a personal job. It is a public office to which any sane person should be able to aspire.

Because of the abuse by Africa's armed forces, our governments spend so much money on killing, torturing and intimidating honest citizens instead of using that money for development.

Collapse of Law:
Collapse of Conscience

Zimbabwe has, indeed, collapsed into anarchy and lawlessness. It is so especially when we see that those who hold public office appear not to know that they are accountable to the people. The government-owned media has become an instrument for delivering daily untruths to its readers and listeners. And the ministers of government seem to have no idea that they have a public responsibility to tell the truth about our political and economic affairs. When such things happen, we know the country is in a state of collapse since those who are supposed to re-awaken public morality and responsibility are determined not to do so.

I believe that corruption begins with the corruption of language. If a senior politician uses vulgar language in public, that is the beginning of corruption (and I am not talking about the other senior politician who likened the people of Zimbabwe to baboons). Once language degenerates into a vehicle for untruth, people are engulfed in a form of corruption.

Our politicians say that the Abuja agreement[1] will be followed to the letter, while ordinary people are being told that they should forget that 'piece of paper'. Political thugs are advised to continue doing their job. Political intimidation is still the order of the day. And lawlessness reigns throughout the land.

African rulers live under the illusion that every citizen is a moron, a fool who will believe anything as long as it is in the newspapers or on television. Every political and business leader should realise, however, that ordinary people understand their own experience and know what they want. They know pain when they see it. They know hunger when they feel it. They know misery when they experience it. And they are able to tell the difference between a liar and an honest person.

Currently we are being told there is no violence in the country, but every day we see our own children being beaten, even killed, and our parents humiliated. Every day we have new widows and new orphans, and they are the result of political lies and murder.

The 'piece of paper' agreed to in Abuja is no more than that. The SADC ministers are living in dreamland if they think Zimbabwean politicians believe a word of what they say in public. Malawi's president, Bakili Muluzi, is living in a fool's paradise if he thinks our politicians will do what they say. No amount of external pressure will make them behave responsibly.

Corruption begins with the corruption of language. Recently people of foreign origin were called 'people without totems'. People of Malawian and Zambian origins have suffered the worst fate on the invaded farms. Some of them came to Zimbabwe over four decades ago. They are as Zimbabwean as anyone else. But now with the chaotic resettlement programme, we are being told that 'those people' never contributed anything to this country; that they did not work hard on the farms or the mines, which brought this country so much wealth. Today Zimbabwe's economic base is being destroyed, and quickly.

Consider what all those ordinary people 'without totems' have done for this country: the footballers, lawyers, thinkers, plantation workers... Like me, they want no more than to breathe fresh, honest, political air. They want neither the violence or the public abuse.

They have no totems and so they will be victimised, or so Zimbabwean political thinking would have it. Our politicians, despite having been supported by the people of surrounding countries in times of need, now suffer total amnesia.

That the so-called war veterans are allowed to run the country like their own chicken farm is shameful. Have the politicians, for reasons of power, forgotten that every Zimbabwean contributed to the liberation struggle in their own way? Those who were working in the city did what they could to keep the villagers supplied with money in order to support the war effort with food and clothes for the guerrillas. The city provided a safe haven when the countryside became too hot. And city-dwellers have not asked for compensation. Support for the struggle was a duty dictated to us by conscience.

In the rural areas villagers were left without a chicken to their name. They sacrificed their all to feed and shelter 'the children of the soil'. The rural businessmen, agricultural officials, nurses and teachers were often pillars of the struggle. And yet, today, they are rubbished by the so-called war veterans.

Today, nurses have to escape to go and clean other people's bottoms in foreign lands. Teachers, too, have to flee the anger of the so-called war veterans and politicians to find work in foreign cities where the education of children means providing them with the values of human dignity and the sanctity of life.

Our ruling politicians have no conscience. None. The death of a nation begins with the death of morality on the part of its leaders and thinkers. A shameless nation visibly dies every day. Decay of the human body begins with the decay of some small part of it. And this is how it is in Zimbabwe. Violence and lawlessness will not end until our politicians examine their consciences and re-shape their sense of public morality and responsibility. You may think violence is sweet if you are on the right end of it. But if you happen to be its victim, you will never use it for political gain, unless you have eaten the herb of eternal forgetfulness.

But people take different things from the same experience. Some former political prisoners know that sending people to prison for their political beliefs was and still is evil. Others vow that when they have power, they will torture and kill in the same fashion as their oppressors.

Our ruling politicians should know that a nation without a sense of shame is a nation that is dying. Our ministers do not respect the truth, but no one tells them to leave office. Senior public officials vow to uphold the law, but their oath is meaningless. And so the nation becomes a nation of crooks and criminals. The message from our leaders is that it is not necessary to live in truth.

As for me, I know I live in a country run by liars who have taken it upon themselves to cheat the people and destroy the national conscience. I know how painful it is to be led by politicians without a national vision and a moral imagination. They conceive of nothing but the fear of losing power; they have no vision for Zimbabwe or its people. We were all once beautiful dreamers, we had hopes for our country, but now we have woken up to the ugliness of nightmare. We live in an ugly political system devoid of human dignity and conscience.

❧ Culture as Censorship ❧

I was born under this blue sky, in the year of the railway line, somewhere under the shadows of the Zvishavane hills, in a mud hut, with no nurse nearby. I only came to know about nurses in primary school: the nurse was the one with sharp needles for anti-this and anti-that. We did not have to know what the inoculations were for. They were part of life, and it went on from sunrise to sunset and from sunset to sunrise.

Our world is measured in many ways: some measure it in sunsets, some in clock-time, some in moons. But we measure time by events. If when you were born nothing else happened, then your birth might be a difficult yardstick. A good birth lies in relation to something important. The railway line was important. And we went there, me and my brothers and cousins, who were born around that time, to the railway line, to check the dates of our births.

To talk literacy and illiteracy is irrelevant. Our parents had their own multi-literacy in many things we did not understand. We were illiterate, young and fresh. Many things still to know and discover, including the kick of a donkey, his mark still visible on my face. (As it happens, I was nearly buried, having been unconscious for longer than the villagers could accept. I'm only alive, thanks to my mother who persuaded them to allow me another day.)

As we grew up, we were told to be wary of a certain two men who always wanted to play with us and offered us sweets. Only now do we realise that they were gay. My relatives would turn in their graves at the thought. To write about those characters is to let slip the ugly face of the village. Every village wants to be portrayed as beautiful, a place into which you were lucky to be born. Thus, cultural pride becomes cultural censorship.

What, after all, is censorship? Is it not the control of local ideas to stop them spreading from the private parts of the village to the public parts of the country? And what is culture? Is it not the things we tell ourselves, the things we pretend to ourselves, about the ways we live and die. Culture is the way we eat, or do not eat, the way we die or do not want to die, the way we talk to the dead to allow for communication between the living and the dead. Even the way we play represents some form of our culture.

But the masks change with time, the ways we eat change with time, and the voices with which we name ourselves change with time. Culture does not exist in a museum. Tradition can.

And the story goes on.

How many of us can write an erotic piece? No, we would shy away from the public glare. Can we write of the body of a woman or of a man, in all its sexuality? We cannot do so because people, in this part of the world, will say, this does not happen in our culture. Isn't culture sometimes a lie with which we all concur? Imagine a woman, in these lands, writing poetry about the love she has for a man. She would be in such trouble that she would wish she had never gone to school or learned to write.

An Indian scholar described power as 'a desolating pestilence', meaning that power can be an instrument of censorship. Power is a cultural tool and the way people relate to it is crucial for the development of the imagination, the mind, the heart, and the soul.

In Zimbabwe today, power is used as violence. Violence has become part of our culture. Violence opposes freedom but the human mind and heart need freedom if they are to bloom.

Ask George Mujajati about it. He is the most tortured writer in this country at the moment. He cannot sleep in peace in his own house. And the violence against him means he is supposed to fall silent, to disappear as it were. When local politicians announce death to those who do not support the ruling party, this is sad news for the imagination.

Religion can also be used as an instrument of censorship. The religious sometimes have the audacity to think that everyone must see the world as they see it themselves. Anybody who does not share their beliefs is considered a heathen, a devil, and thus the literary imagination is controlled. For, censorship has to do with controlling the imaginations and products of other people's imagination in an attempt to make the world uniform, monocultural, and mono-everything else.

We can talk of language as censorship because it is an instrument of life. Language tends to be harnessed by those who think they own the social imagination. Language is culture and culture is communication. Silence is not culture. Without communication, all the doors of human existence and human exchange are closed and locked, as Mujajati says in *The Sun Will Rise Again*:[2] 'Culture is an instrument of aspiration and dream. Within it, the dreams of the ordinary person may live or die.'

Violence inflicted on people can mean the death of creativity.

✥ Freedom and Knowledge ✥

Violence is a serious form of censorship. 'Vote for me or else I will kill you! I will go back to war. I have guns hidden all over the place,' threatens a so-called liberator. There are not many who will stand up to his threat, especially if they have experienced political violence before. Violence may be a threat to your psychological person as well as your physical person: physically you may be threatened with death, psychologically your freedom of thought, your knowledge and your experience are threatened because they are invalidated and diminished.

Illiteracy is a form of censorship. Our country is run in the English language. Too bad for those who do not understand it. Road signs, bank transactions, legal documents are all in English. Even parliamentary speeches by our semi-literate honourable members of parliament are in English.

The idea is to block the peasantry out of the country's official systems and institutions. Radio Two broadcasts programmes which suggest that the planners think that all villagers are concerned about is to send messages to their far-flung relatives or to express their fear of the witches that invade their homes.

Peasant farmers are made to believe that they are dealing with the Cotton Company and other players competing to buy cotton grown from the hard soil and nurtured by their weathered hands. Issues of the rights or wrongs of such monopolies are not discussed in our own languages. The implication is that such issues are too complicated for villagers to understand. It means that when 'back pay' time comes, the peasant farmers will be so grateful to the company for buying from them at their price that they will sell their produce to the same company again next season.

The politicians provide statistics about how many people can read even when we know that many of them only had a primary school education and never had access to books thereafter. They may no longer even be able to read and write. The roads to new ideas through books and broadcasting are all closed. Entertainment and propaganda is the order of the day. This suits the government. No questions asked.

I am the son of a farmer who grew cotton, maize and sunflowers. I knew how to drive a tractor when I was fourteen. I discovered, through hard experience, that the joy which bloomed on my father's face when the crops where ready for harvest soon dried up when he knew that the destination of his harvest was not for him to know. His crops shaped the destinies of others. Keeping people in ignorance is a form of censorship – a powerful one.

The physical road along which buses and donkey carts travel provides a form of censorship. Buses carry people. People carry ideas. The best way to keep the nation ignorant is to deprive them of roads so that new ideas do not cross certain boundaries. That is why the ruling party's strategy has often included beating up those who were able to move from the city to country with ease. They carried new ideas, they carried information about the new prices of cooking oil and sugar.

Knowledge cleanses the mind of fear. It clears the mini states of emergency which reside in the heart. But knowledge alone is not enough. It needs a dash of wisdom, and another dash of humility. *'Gudo guru peta muswe, vaduku vagokuremekedza,'* (Big baboon fold your tail in humility so that the small baboons can respect you.)

We all have multiple identities. We are poly-cultural. We became cultural coloureds as soon as we met others from other lands, and they did too. We found different yardsticks to judge ourselves and others. Through a combination of knowledge and wisdom, we soon discover that there is ugliness and beauty in everyone. Our human choice is to judge what should be allowed to dominate: the gold in us, or the dross in us. The rainbows of our hearts should not be clouded by the dust of wilful ignorance. No nation deserves that.

There are those who think that they own the truth, the only truth; and others who believe that truth is a mirage. I tend to side with the latter. There is no one absolute truth in the world. As a writer, I have discovered that to write is to search for many veins of truth, many streams of knowledge, to discover the confluence of ideas, and to live and write them as an expression of my human freedom.

True knowledge is a struggle against personal and collective impotence. To unfold the various layers of reality is to conquer impotence at all levels. Sometimes our media tries to make us all feel impotent. The media in this country is the mouthpiece of those that think there is only one truth – their own. Illusions are touted to the general public as reality. Democracy begins to be measured in the corpses littering the political streets.

But knowledge is a weapon of liberation, and wisdom is a better one. The hypocrite is a prisoner of his own untruths, machinations or lies. An honest knowledgeable person is a free person who will humbly search for freedom for others, not for himself.

The rich and politically powerful say: to know is good, but to have is better.

The wise if politically weak say: to have is good, but to know the dangers of power is better.

🐾 Liberty, Express Thyself 🐾

Recently I was travelling far away from home. As usual, I decided to have a social drink. But it wasn't much fun because as soon as someone discovered that I was from Zimbabwe, their face fell. We all know why. In the end, if I wanted to enjoy my drink and enjoy the local company, I told people that I came from Togo. Only then did the discussion develop into something one could call a dialogue. Zimbabwe has a battered image: Zimbabweans have become the laughing stock of the world. Yet we were once proud to come from a country that was, as Julius Nyerere said, 'The pearl of Africa'. A small country shaped like a human heart; a small but dynamic economy; a hard-working, creative people.

Every day we read of people being beaten while the police stand by; of the army threatening people with guns, of ministers uttering threats. This is the new policy. I feel ashamed. When a government decides to defend itself against its own people, you know there is something amiss.

There are many ways of expressing yourself in a democracy. You should have no need to fear. A silent people is a dead nation. To talk is to shape your own destiny. To be silent is to resign your fate to others. Silence! Death! Non-language. We are told, 'Newspapers must be banned.' Ideas must suffer. *Nhai veduwee!* (Oh, what is this, my people?) Why are posters removed from the streets because they said something about liberty and self-expression? *Ah! Ah! Ah! Ah! Haikona!* No, this is not the way to handle freedom. It is dictatorship.

What is wrong with expressing oneself? Voices are for self-expression. That is why we have different voices, all of us, in the orchestra of democracy. Clothes are for self-expression. You wear this and I wear that. We express ourselves. To express yourself is to talk, to announce that you are there, in the world created for you by the gods.

There is no democracy in silence. The leaders of our country must know this. Democracy is about shouting out loudly when your rights have been abused. Silence is death. A lack of communication is also death.

Our president has to walk in the city and meet people who will tell him how he is mismanaging the country. It is a gentleman's agreement. Walk and talk to the electorate.

The fear of freedom is dictatorship. In a dictatorship, people must be subdued. There must be silence. Words are forbidden. Ideas are killed in broad daylight. Dictatorships are known for manufacturing technologies of torture. The first thing repressed is ideas. Then follows the elimination of the producers of those ideas.

Now, why would a government be afraid of a thinking people? First, to think is to act. To act is to think, under normal circumstances. To avoid thinking is to decay. Let us say a nation goes for twenty-four hours without thinking. What would happen?

Liberty, express thyself, freely!

The fear of freedom is the beginning of foolishness. A government that fears freedom is leading its people into foolishness. Why did someone decide that a poster with a slogan about liberty and self-expression was not acceptable in a country that proclaims to be free?

'Freedom or death' was the slogan coined by General Sandino of Nicaragua. To be denied freedom is to die. Every person feeds on freedom or the illusion of it. Even the prisoner lives under the illusion that one day he will be free. That alone is enough to keep him alive in prison.

The other day I was writing about how we have become a police state, just as in the old days of 'good old Smithie'; but Ian Smith made no bones about it while our own people's government pretends all is well. *Bakhiti!* (Guys!) But now we have armed police, armed war veterans, guns all over the place. We even have a Rapid Reaction Force on the alert to react against people who might choose to express their freedom.

Many years ago, I advocated a huge conference to discuss fear and ways of removing it. Fear is in our minds as we deal with our daily routines. If you talk of the rise of food prices, the person sitting next to you in the bus might tell you to 'hush' or your next destination will be prison. If you talk about the blunders that our executive president has made, the guy sitting next to you will say he doesn't need to be told, he knows them as well as you do, but he does not want to go to Chikurubi maximum security prison.

We need a long public discussion on fear and how to remove it from our minds. That way democracy will flourish, ideas too. Look at the amount of theft around us today. How much of this has to do with the fact that people have been silenced?

Liberty, express yourself.

The president of a democracy should know that the public is watching everything he does on a daily basis. That is a measure of what the people expect from the president. If they do not get what they need and want, they must protest. This is liberty.

'Express yourself' should actually be the slogan of every democracy. How else can you live? Imagine a country of mute people. Saying nothing, doing nothing, hearing nothing. A dead nation.

No doubt it would have a ruler who acted as if the people who elected him did not exist.

Democracy is about continuous dialogue. Democracy does not mean voting someone into power and forgetting about them until the next election. Six years of forgetting is a long time and a lot can happen in this time, especially when people are silent. *Chokwadi!* Truly, democracy means listening to the voter all the time, and maintaining an open discussion. He who chooses public office must be prepared to engage with the public on everything. The good democrat is one who is prepared to sit under a tree and talk with villagers about the economy, the political situation of the nation, the distribution of power, the prices of crops, the introduction of French in schools, HIV/AIDS. Everything!

The first and last thing to remember is that the electorate has the power. The politicians are only messengers. Their job is to run up and down between parliament and their constituency, reporting back, seeking advice, finding out what men, women and children think, going to and fro on a full-time basis.

The political journey begins with just one voter.

❧ Zimbabwe's Lost Visions ☙

Twenty years of independence is time enough to assess our successes and failures; to give ourselves an evaluation. Our national problem, of course, is that we have only allowed politicians themselves to assess their misdeeds and their five-year plans, which usually coincide with parliamentary and presidential terms. However, the nation lives beyond election periods.

Every country has a take-off point. It is like a train station. But if you miss the train, you've missed it. Remember Nigeria. It had an oil boom that provided a great opportunity to turn itself into a rich developed country. Instead the politicians and businessmen saw it as an opportunity to enrich only themselves. They stole and stole again, so the country lost its chance to develop. The people were left behind.

Zimbabwe also had its take-off point, just after independence in the early 1980s. There was then so much goodwill among the citizenry that you could have asked all working people to donate a week's pay to a national cause and they would have gladly done it. There was so much national energy and such vision that if it had been properly mobilised we would have travelled a long way as a nation.

Take education, for example. There was such a thirst for it that we almost succeeded in having every child in school. Adults also heeded the call. They invaded night schools and adult literacy classes all over the country. Secondary schools turned out thousands every year. Children and their families invested energy and money to realise the dream of a school certificate, which would, they hoped, provide a ticket to a new and better future. People had dreams and they took them seriously, they wanted to shape their own destiny.

But the train of state missed that station. Education was provided, sometimes half-baked. But whether young people left school with or without a certificate, there was nothing for them to do. The result: unemployment, frustration, desperation, crime. So, parents have lost confidence in our education system. And, for the first time, we have unemployed graduates, young people who have been taught to think.

Lost visions. Lost opportunities. Another junction missed in our walk to freedom. This is now one of the reasons why Zimbabwean politicians hate the so-called 'born frees'.

The free-born are a special people. They detest being dosed with historical rhetoric. They want to live for the present and the future. They are not responsible for the past and they don't want it forced down their throats. Give them the future, and their hands will be full. *Matakadya kare haanyaradzi mwana.* (That you ate many years ago does not finish the hunger of a starving child today.)

One thing, however, that Zimbabweans will never lack is slogans. 'Education for all by the year 2000', 'Health for all by the year 2000', 'Housing for all by the year 2000', 'Vision 2020'. And so forth and so on. All of which came to nought. We overlooked the fact that every vision needs a serious plan about how it will be paid for and implemented.

Zimbabwe used to have a sound economy to which everyone wanted to contribute. Workers were prepared to work. Teachers were willing to give extra lessons without asking for extra pay. Nurses did not nurse to the clock. They cared for their patients in a humane way.

But look at where we are now. The national goodwill has been destroyed. You see a nurse knitting a jersey while she is on duty. You see a teacher minding a tuckshop from the classroom. The chairman of a housing co-operative is highly likely to have helped himself to the funds entrusted to him. Politician think of the national coffers as their personal funds to use as and when they wish. Importers and exporters import and export so little, how can they help the economy to grow?

Destruction is easy, construction takes time and serious plans.

Unfortunately, our politicians have become some kind of 'demolition squad'. I was shocked when a politician told me: 'A country never goes broke as long as it has the land.' All I could say was: 'The land becomes economic only if the owner knows how to make it produce, and people know how to turn the produce into secondary goods; fruit into jam, cotton into cloth, trees into paper, and so on. ' As you can imagine, this cut no ice with the politician who is no doubt happy to see our forests, which have taken hundreds of years to grow, turned into firewood overnight.

As it is, the Zimbabwean economy has collapsed. No amount of land grabbing or fast-track resettlement will revive it.

Now we know that politicians believe that African economies never collapse until there is no food in state house. We have to seriously re-think our political and economic destiny and only we can do this, it is not something to be left to stale politicians whose tenure has benefited themselves and no one else.

ஃ Palaver Finish ஃ

You go see a man walk in de street. You tink de man got it in de head. De man drop a ting, a bad and a small one. You go give shout and say to de man, man, you drop a ting like dis and go walk walk walk. What is dis? De man turn to you and give punch.

Palaver finish.

De laziest animal on dis god-given eart is a man. He go no produce milk. He go no sell vegetables on the market. He go no produce eggs. He go eat eat eat. Ah, I go mean politician. He no produce nutting. He go eat everyting dat you and I produce. He go no sell vegetables on the market. All he go do is palaver palaver palaver. Talk talk talk go no sell vegetable on the market. Palaver go no bring food in de house.

Palaver finish.

De political man go have big belly and big appetite. He no worker. He no produce nutting. But surprise is dat if you go talk to de political man about sensible ting, he go get angry wit you. He go come for you troat and want chop it for you. You ask question, he tell you no question till after you go die. What is dat?

De uder day, I go talk politics wit de man standing for me in de palaver house, de one dey call parliament. De man go get angry wit me and hire a few palaver men to beat me finish. I go say: 'Hey, me be citizen. Me be constituent and voter.' De man look me in de face and spit. You know, giving me spit in de face! No! De man he go go too far. Spit in de face!

Palaver finish.

Palaver go no sell vegetable in de market. Palaver go bring no income. Palaver finish!

Dey go say a man be as foolish as de man can show himself to be. Me no foolish man. A silent foolish man is a good man. A palaver foolish man is a palaver dangerous man. A silent politician witout palaver is a wise man. Politician with too much palaver is dangerous man.

Politician stop me in de street. He go look bad and angry and ugly. Me I go look and put a fake smile.

'Hey you, what you tink about de president and the country?' he go say.

'Me, palaver finish,' I go say. 'Me got no have pinion at all. In dis country opinion is bad. Palaver finish,' I go say. De man go shout shout and curse and curse.

Palaver finish.

De oder day, I go meet anoder politician. He tink tink too much, with a little hair on his head. He go palaver palaver again. About food and riot.

'Me got no opinion on food. Me got no opinion on beverages either. Me got no opinion on riots. But I can tell you someting, riot kill, police hungry too, police kill, army kill, central intelligent kill, everybody kill,' and de man walk away, feeling angry wit me, an ordinary foolish man who cannot even write good English.

At de party congress, anoder man ask me what I go tink about transport. 'Which transport?' I go ask. 'De is no transport around,' I go say. He punch me in de face and I ask him why, not wit words, but with a stronger punch. He look me in face and get surprise. I walk away.

Palaver finish!

Assault assault assault. Verbal assault be no harm. Physical assault be bad! Anoder man assault me de oder day. He say: 'Hey you, if de president invite you to cabinet like he did to Jonatan, what you go be?'

I say to de man, go guess. He guess wrong again.

'You be minister of culture. You good wit de white man's language,' he go tink.

'But I go tink in village language. I go no tink at all,' I go say.

De man look me, and I go remind him: 'Dis time you wrong. I be minister of agriculture or finance. Me go practice culture too long. A doctor is de most worst minister of healt you can have. He go know all all about medicine. He go bully bully all about de ministry,' I go say.

Palaver finish. Palaver go no sell vegetable in de market.

De oder day, a man go ask me what I be tink about footbaal. I go say me no play footbaal. He go say, 'Hey, tink about footbaal. It is good for your healt.' I tink tink tink.

'No, man, footbaal go be dictatorship, man,' I go say.

De man go be surprise.

'What you go talk oh about footbaal? Footbaal nutting to do wit dictatorship. You go be understand?' de man go say.

'You go see my man, I be speak. Footbaal be dictatorship,' I go tell de man.

'What you go be mean oh?' de man say.

'Footbaal, one dictator plus two assistant dictator,' I go answer oh. 'De refree be dictator wit two assistant dictator, controlling dem twenty-two players and sixty tousand crowd. De man be dictator and I go see dat I tink it a rehearsal for one president and de two

vice president. It de rehearsal for de one-party state. Me no like it,'
I go talk free free. De man want give punch on my face. I go say no.
Dis time, a small punch for a big punch. You go punch me once I
go punch you twice, heavy too!' I go tell de man. He fright and run
away after see the size of me punch.

'Me, I understand politics,' de man go say.

'Me live politics' I go say.

Palaver finish.

De ting is dat de is too much people who go tink dey clever and
know much. If you go ask dem about simple ting, dey know nutting.
Nutting. Dey know no direction of de wind. Dey know no plan of
de city. Dey know de bird has no feader but it can fly.

Oh, de old man say, in his palaver house, ignorance be expensive.
You be ask any politician about de matter.

Palaver finish. Me go no talk talk anymore.

Palaver finish.

You go talk wit me about Kabila deat. Me I go refuse. Me no kill
Kabila. Me no be killed on behalf of Kabila. Kabila be no uncle of
mine. Kabila be no broder of mine. Kabila go no sell vegetable in
de market.

Palaver finish.

You go ask me about de judge. I go say me no man of law. But
talk dat de judge be appointed by de president. And I go say, de
president be angry angry too much wit de judge. Me no involve.
Me no man of law. De president be man of law. Me no no no!

You go see, palaver finish! Palaver go no sell vegetable in de
market. Politician go no sell anyting to anybody.

Politician be have problem. Me, no problem. Zimbabwean
politician be dictator. Me, no problem. De politician be power power
power too much. De peasant, like me, be no power.

Palaver finish!

ఎ Party Symbols ఎ

West Africans have a story of a man who, when his house caught fire was seen running after the rats fleeing the flames. He had such an appetite for his task that his neighbours watched in disbelief. They did not bother to help him by putting out the fire.

We have a similar story, that of a learned parliamentarian who, in the middle of a serious fuel shortage and an unprecedented economic crisis, tried to introduce a motion to ban the MDC[3] open-hand symbol. One wonders how such people get elected to parliament. Do they not know that parliament is a serious national debating chamber?

The gentleman in question has a Master of Philosophy degree or the equivalent. It seems his philosophy is to tell the people of this country what the open palm should or should not mean to them. He might do better to tell us all the meaning of *jongwe*, the cockerel, the ZANU(PF) symbol, as well as that of the clenched fist. Following his paradigm, perhaps he would say that people should feel frightened every time they kill a rooster to celebrate some festive occasion. PF ZAPU chose the bull as their symbol. Our philosopher did not tell the nation that everyone who owned a bull was insulting the ruling party. No, he was silent.

The problem that we face in Zimbabwe is one of small-talk. No one is ashamed of talking nonsense at a time when we need serious argument and debate. In the old days, those who engaged in chit-chat in the presence of elders were asked to go and skin a goat a long way away from the serious proceedings. '*Ngaaende anovhiya mbudzi yedare uyo*,' the wise elders declared. (Let him go and skin the goat to be eaten by this court).

Everyone knows that ZANU(PF) was caught unawares by the opposition. Recall the incident when the ruling party asked what was 'in the other hand' when the MDC introduced the open palm. They even advertised the question. The opposition party wittily responded that what was in the other hand was a red card signifying that the ruling party should leave the field. The moral is don't ask silly questions.

Just because you are in politics doesn't mean you have to lose your sense of humour. I remember hearing about an angry English woman who threw a number of rotten eggs at the then Labour Prime Minister, Harold Wilson. The British leader was quick off the mark: 'Having a Labour government' he quipped, 'must mean that you have so many eggs you can afford to throw them away!' Who had the last laugh?

If you have a wild imagination, you might figure out what would happen if it our own President got pelted with rotten eggs. Someone might become the object of a gun rather than a joke.

Who said politics should be devoid of laughter? The problem with our politicians is that they take their status so seriously that they no longer know how to laugh at themselves. The capacity to laugh at yourself shows a certain level of maturity which is needed if we have to survive and develop. Because our government lacks a sense of humour, our political leaders will never appreciate the jokes made about them. They are wrapped in the blanket of a long political night.

African politicians are not ashamed of lying in public. They repeat the same lies so often that they believe them. The basis of their untruths is that they consider that peasants and workers have no idea of how they want to shape their destiny. Our politicians assume they are The Great Leaders of a hapless people, and are full of self-congratulation, but what really have they achieved in the name of the people?

The other day, a good friend said: 'If they ban the MDC's open hand symbol, what will happen if the opposition party chooses a smile as its next symbol? Will the whole nation be banned from smiling? After all, they have tried to stop us waving.'

Soon tongues (because they are red like the MDC red card) will be banned. All red cloth, red shirts, red dresses, red zambias will be banned, because according to the thinking of the minister of propaganda, they are symbols of opposition.

In order to remove this problem of the open palm from the public domain, why doesn't the minister chop off our hands so that there will be no palms to wave at each other? That will solve the problem once and for all. We will become a nation of handless people. Next he can cut out our tongues, so we become a nation of silent people. Imagine! But let not the madness end there. Let him order us all to keep roosters. The sound of crowing will fill the air instead of the sound of voices.

What a wonderful country it will be!

Untruth upon untruth. If the ruling party thinks that racism is a card to use in gaining votes, why don't they lead by example? The Minister of Health (or Death) is not the same colour as me. Why don't they fire him and tell the nation that they no longer wish to play with anyone who is not the same colour as our president or minister of propaganda?

The citizens of the land are quick to notice all these strains of hypocrisy that are paraded as nationalism. Lawlessness, thuggery, murder, intimidation, racism, torture and cruelty are now engulfing the nation as if they were something to be proud of. And all in the name of subduing Zimbabweans until they resign their fate to some heartless, humourless politician.

All our politicians must realise that we have a larger and longer destiny than one that is measured in political terms of office. We and our progeny will live here for thousands of years to come. Why don't our self-styled leaders remember that long after they are dead, the country will remain, and it will harbour memories of what they have done to innocent people who only had something to say?

We know that power really drives people mad. This is not fiction. It is the truth. And the kind of power that we are enduring has ruined our country. To recover from this political and economic damage will take us many many long years.

ꙮ Africa: Reality and Imagination ꙮ

A few years ago, flying from Washington DC to London, the American airline showed us a short documentary about the planet earth. Each continent was identified by the level of development it had achieved. Use of electricity was one of the criteria of development. In terms of availability of electricity per square kilometre, Africa is still 'the dark continent' we were told.

The concept of the dark continent is very old, and it is rooted in the West. It evokes images of the primitive, of wanton violence, neglect of the poor, disease, and fiscal indiscipline. African leaders are projected as corrupt: reckless big spenders who drive in a Mercedes Benz while their villages don't even boast a decent footpath. Sadly the few leaders who do try to run their countries in the spirit of democracy and social justice, have to overcome the stereotype of the African dictator.

It must be said that we inherited violence, prisons, handcuffs and guns from the West after they had destroyed our own institutions. Our post-colonial leaders came to power with instruments of repression firmly established. And now they smile the whole way to the torture chambers where their supposed 'enemies' will be annihilated. Is this the reason Africa, to Europe, is still a dark continent because its natural disasters, military coups, cruel dictators, senseless civil wars and droves of refugees, dominate the European imagination?

For there is hypocrisy in this perception. When I wrote an article for a Swedish magazine on my perceptions of the new Europe, the editor protested against my use of the phrase, 'the tribes of Europe are at war with each other again'. He preferred 'ethnic groups' to 'tribes'. I refused to change my terminology. When Africa is at war, the conflict is called tribal. But when the war takes place in Kosovo, the warring parties are called 'ethnic Albanians' or 'ethnic Serbs'. In Shona, we say: *'Dindingwe rinonaka richakweva rimwe, kana iro rokwehwa roti mavara angu azara vhu.'* (A cheetah is happy dragging another one in the dust, but when its own turn to be dragged comes, it complains about its spots being soiled.)

The politics and power of language put Africa at the receiving end, not least because our business is always conducted in languages which are not the ones in which we first named the trees, birds, rivers and mountains of our geographical and psycho-emotional landscapes.

When people talk of the global village, Africa does not seem to be at the centre of that village. But a village is a human settlement in which everyone knows and cares about everyone else. Our global village simply allows others to peep into our homes while we cannot peep into theirs. Technology peeps into our houses from afar, while we cannot technologically correct the information that is put out about ourselves. We are at the receiving end of information from the West, it does not work the other way around.

Once while teaching in the United States, my tenure came to an end. It was the time of the Rwanda genocide. My students had no idea about Africa or the size of the continent, so they all contributed money and requested the President of the university to allow me to stay on in case I was killed on my return to Africa. I had to give them back their money and explain that Zimbabwe was nowhere near Rwanda.

So, a disaster in Sudan is a disaster in Botswana, according to such perceptions. Imagine a student seriously asking me if Zimbabwe was in Victoria Falls. And when you say that Zimbabwe is three times the size of the United Kingdom, they giggle and stare as if you were a serious liar.

Africa is the most humorous continent on earth. At the time of the Rwanda disaster, I saw pictures of men, women and children, still able to muster a smile in the midst of terrible carnage and suffering. In Africa, we laugh in order not to cry. Whatever happens, we keep on hoping beyond hope and dreaming of the future. As long as there is breath in our bodies, we believe in the endurance of the human spirit.

And because we maintain our humour despite our problems, we are thought funny; and we are certainly not considered commercially minded. We are perceived as charlatans of the economic and technological world stage. Instead of accepting the beauty of the human soul in our humour, our laughter, we are told that we are not serious. Our music and dance form another expression of African resilience, though musicians are sometimes criticised for being too political. So on the one hand we are criticised for laughing in the face of tragedy, while on the other, we are criticised for being too political. This is also true of our literature. It is still sometimes said that the business of literature has nothing to do with politics and that literature from Africa is too political. But if African writers are too political, what of Shakespeare, or Victor Hugo or D. H. Lawrence?

Part of the problem of western perception is that the teaching of geography has been dropped in favour of science and technology. Even African literature is often reserved for students of social anthropology, like material from the curio shop. And sadly those that come here, often come for the wrong reasons. Tourists come to Africa to see The Big Five: the rhino, elephant, lion, buffalo, and leopard. Instead they should come to see The Big Heart, that is our people who are the centre of everything. To see Great Zimbabwe and Victoria Falls can never be enough: the people are the most beautiful part of our emotional and historical landscape.

I am told the West is dealing with the issue of empowerment. Empowerment simply means the ability to harness and develop the capacity to shape one's own destiny. A people without that capacity will perish as other people will interpret their dreams for them.

Let the West come and see us among our elephants, birds and flowers, our rivers, our skies, our sad joyful sunsets and sunrises, our smoke-filled huts beaming with struggle and hope. Let the West come and see total context of our lives as we struggle on in the interpretation of our own aspirations and dreams in pursuit of our own African destinies and identities.

That should be the basis of our interaction with others, now and always.

❧ The New Millenium in the Village ❧

After the Bikita West by-elections, it is sensible to conclude that in Zimbabwe the villager is an endangered species. Poor villager, when he has been convinced that we are in the new millenium and he believes it, at election time he is dragged back to the Dark Ages. The same politician who wants to 'develop' the villager is the same one who shows the peasant that he is the most 'under-developed' human being on earth.

Defenceless, and isolated in his own homestead, the young boys and girls employed to kill will arrive at any time and kill the villager and his family. He is lucky if he is beaten and left for dead. Maybe he will find someone to take him to the clinic on a donkey cart.

Political violence leaves the villager weaker than he has ever been in his life. Of course, he is already weak in all areas of human activity in this new millenium. The old century came and left him illiterate, economically weak, and politically isolated. The country is run in the English language, which he does not understand. To him, the new millenium is a marvel. He does not see the difference at all.

Under normal circumstances, he would have expected to be respected as a human being, a citizen, a parent and a voter. But no, the way he was beaten up during the war of liberation is just the same as the way he was maimed and tortured for his vote in 2001. Actually, the villager soon discovers the black leaders are the worst torturers of them all. The white man was, to the lone villager, a much better torturer than the 'liberators'.

Just imagine two villagers, neighbours in Bikita West or even in Lupane. They were told that the country was free. They are free like everyone else. Many of them have attended political and development rallies about this isssue of freedom. They were told that they can now exercise their democratic right to choose who they want to stand for them in parliament.

Old man Makusha is busy carving a wooden stool. Old man Moyo is busy weaving an *ilala* mat.

'Moyo, this time our new party is going to beat yours,' Makusha challenges his friend.

'Wait until the voting time comes. I am going to tell everyone about my old party, our new ways of doing things. We will win,' Moyo amuses himself. And they laugh together as they have always done for many years as neighbours and friends.

Two weeks later, when election time comes, the youth from Makusha's party arrive with sticks and stones. They burn Moyo's huts and granaries before beating him up, and forcing him to perform all sorts of shameful acts in front of his children and wife.

Meanwhile, Moyo's power-hungry party leaders have their hit list, which includes Makusha. They arrive at his home and burn all his huts, including the fowl-run, before beating him until he is almost dead.

Anger and hatred form scars in the hearts of the two villagers who have been friends for so long.

And when the violent young people have gone to attend some politician's election 'victory', the two are no longer 'neighbours'. One wants to poison the other, or at least to kill the other's chickens, goats, cattle and children. And shamelessly, the politicians speak of unity after they have disrupted and divided the smallest unit which forms the basis of our national unity.

Moyo decides to move to another part of the country, to start a new life where he hopes another Makusha will not emerge to victimise him by using youths imported from some strange place elsewhere.

Violence fragments long-standing relations in the villages. During elections, villagers wonder why armed youths, the police, the army and certain other mysterious men and women come to threaten them with death, if they don't vote in a particular way. Our so-called war veterans call themselves 'liberators' but it does not make sense to 'liberate' people from one oppressor so that you become their new oppressor.

Political choices can only be made in a free atmosphere in which voters go to the polls with a certain sense of self-respect and human dignity. What we have seen in Bikita West and many other constituencies is really political barbarism and vulgarity.

Some people say politics are dirty. But I think that if the politicians are not prepared to clean their politics up, it is they who are dirty. To a sane man or woman, there is a wide gap between political barbarism and political campaigning. So far we have been subjected to political barbarism by shameless politicians who then celebrate their 'victory' over other people's corpses.

African politics is always marred by a dangerous obsession with power and money. Our problem is that Zimbabwean and other African politicians enter politics not for the service they want to give to the nation, but to make money. European politicians enter politics in order to extend their financial power to other spheres. Not so with African politicians. They enter politics with nothing in their hands, and in a few months they are millionaires. Shame! They do not have the shame of looting from a country in which more than half the population cannot read and write. They do not have the shame of stealing from a country where there is no medicine in public hospitals. Shame!

As I have always said, power without conscience is rotten. It stinks. And political power in Zimbabwe really stinks. Someone has to clean it up, otherwise the whole country will go to the vultures.

I saw ugly-hearted politicians celebrating the ruling party's 'victory' in Bikita West. What a shame! There was nothing to celebrate after such damage to the relationships of people in Bikita. Village leaders were being terrorised as if they were children who are told to stand in a line and tell everyone that their people were going to vote for ZANU(PF). In a civilised society, is that freedom of choice?

Dictatorship does not simply start one fine morning. It begins in small places and spreads in long tentacles and grasping reach. What I saw in Bikita West was the workings of a dictatorship in motion, tyranny dished out to every homestead.

The abuse of youths is the beginning of dictatorship. No children of politicians campaigned in Bikita West: no, I am sure their children were happily eating ice-cream in a safe place in the city. The children of the poor are the ones being paid to do their dirty work with whips, sticks and stones.

Women, too, are abused in politics. They have to dance the most. They have to sing the loudest. They are the ones made to denounce their husbands in public. Thus, families are destroyed simply for the love of political power. And then, it is the women who are given the most minor posts when their political party wins elections.

Violence begins with violent language streaming recklessly from the mouths of shameless politicians. Zimbabwe is high on the league of shameless politicians in Africa. But they do not seem to mind because they have no shame. Most Zimbabwean politicians are thugs masquerading as our national saviours. But let us return Zimbabwe to the rule of law and human conscience.

Violence, Tear-gas, Handcuffs and Democracy

A man appears in the newspapers, with a hat that looks like a bird's nest. Whoever wove that contraption for solar protection could never have imagined that it would become a symbol of tyranny worn by the chief commander of farm invasions. He is in the same class as another who publicly proclaimed that he has arms hidden all over the place, which he would be prepared to use if his party loses the elections. These are men who say they understand democracy.

True, democracy is about making demands, not for passive acquiescence, but demands to be heard. You are free to demand to see your Member of Parliament, your councillor, the headmaster of your child's school. You have a right to expect that they listen to you rather than talk at you. Even if you did not go to school for long, you have attended the school of life, the school of the market place.

Somebody has to talk to our politicians to remind them that democracy is about dialogue, not tear-gas and police batons. Nobody knows everything all the time, everywhere. A leader has to develop the capacity to listen. Those who cannot listen have nothing to do with democracy.

Voting means you authorise another person to speak on your behalf. But if that person does not listen to you, how can they talk on your behalf? The usual argument is that the people are not educated, so the leaders have to guide them. The question we must ask is: why would a person want to lead people who are not educated? But if someone has chosen to lead the people, then they must listen to them unconditionally.

I have always said that African leaders prefer to keep their people illiterate because they do not want them to read all the hopeless laws that they make in parliament. Let the people read and they will not accept all the nonsense that is passed into law, and is for no one's benefit except the law-makers'. Remember our parliament once discussed some crazy idea about digging a canal that would carry people from some lake into the city centre? The law-maker had been to Venice! What madness!

Why not make a law that insists that the MP lives in his or her constituency. After all, *sabhuku unotonga kwake ikoko* (the headman rules in his constituency). He has to stay there, listening to both praise and ridicule. He has no choice. He has no other address. That is some form of democracy.

African democracies are measured in corpses, not in the flowers honouring the leader for his or her effective leadership. At the moment, Zimbabwe is how many corpses? And we say we are a democracy. Why does someone have to die for a leader to have power? Some new propagandists say quite happily that our corpses are fewer than those of other countries. *Mhaihwe!* (Oh, my dear mother!) How can we sink so low as to say that our democracy is better because we have fewer corpses than, say, South Africa?

A corpse is a corpse is a corpse. A murderer is a murderer is a murderer. Human life is so precious that you cannot argue that you are better than someone else because you killed fewer people. What a shame! If you are dirty you are dirty – no amount of showing us other dirty people will convince us that you are clean.

Watching Zimbabwe's police and army in action the other day, one could not but be reminded of the police in apartheid South Africa. Their faces are stamped with the language of brutality and mercilessness. We have become a police-army state. One thinks of a Rapid Reaction Force as an army unit designed for defending citizens from foreign invaders. But no! Our Reaction Force is meant to inflict violence on innocent civilians sleeping in their homes, in which they are already suffering as a result of the horrendously mismanaged economy.

I once saw a picture of Idi Amin, the monster of Uganda. His shirt was covered in military medals that he had given himself. I could not help exclaiming: 'So many medals for conquering his own people!' He even gave himself the absurd title of Field Marshall. A Field Marshall of a war to subdue his own people and ruin their economy! Violence, brute force, guns, tear-gas, handcuffs, prisons, instruments to politically subjugate the people! And in a country which claims to be a democracy.

'*Munhu mutema haanzwi. Anofanira kurohwa kuti aite zvaunoda*' (An African is stubborn. He must be beaten in order for him to do what you want), said an African politician. Having a lack of imagination, he had conveniently forgotten that he too was an African. Should he be whacked by the electorate for being stubborn and not doing what the people want?

As a good friend once said, 'Murdering people for their vote is plain bad manners.' Bombing other people's offices is plain bad manners. Beating up people for their vote is plain bad manners. Burning other people's houses for electioneering purposes is plain bad manners. Overturning other people's cars for their vote is bad manners. Anyone with a decent mother will have been told these simple truths at infant grade.

One local politician once quizzed me on why I had not joined the ruling political party that, after all, had 32 million dollars. Of course, democracy should have nothing to do with money, but we all know that there are some people who will do anything to spend that dollar. Plain bad manners again. Didn't your mother tell you about greed? What about 'principle'? The hunger for power is worse than the hunger for food. But, power eats away at conscience.

On the basis of our own experience we could make certain rules about parliamentary governance. Here they are:

- ❖ Parliament is the house of speaking and informed debate, a place to marshall facts and figures in order to convince others of the justness of your argument.
- ❖ Parliament is not a place for lying or cheating.
- ❖ Parliament is a place where people both speak and listen.
- ❖ MPs should always be responsible to their constituents, report back to them and listen to their ideas and opinions.
- ❖ Arrogance should be left at home and not brought into parliament.
- ❖ Taxpayers' money does not belong to one party but is there for the provision of efficient government service.
- ❖ Laws should be made for everyone's benefit and not to suit the ruling party only.
- ❖ Parliament is not a place for people to sleep either literally or metaphorically.
- ❖ MPs are paid salaries out of the taxpayers money. Parliament is not a place to do private business.

Arrogance and democracy are like water and oil. They do not mix. The voter is master. The member of parliament is servant. That is the new relationship in Zimbabwe. No violence or threats of violence. No waving of fists. When you are high up in society, control your language. A Somali proverb states: 'The higher the monkey climbs, the more it exposes its bottom'. Our leaders whether of the ruling party or in the opposition are high up in the tree of power. Beware of exposure!

Whether we like it or not, political parties will always be there. Their mission is to know that *ushe madzoro* (Kingship is taken in turns). We are talking of tolerance. It means Zimbabwean political parties have to recognise and accept that they are going to be sharing the same political space for a long time. Not a single one of them can imagine that they have the right to monopolise that political space.

Intolerance has to do with greed. If there is a plateful of food, the greedy man or woman grabs it and says it is theirs. The tolerant one invites others to come and share his plate so all can go home satisfied. Corruption is a serious form of greed. Trying to eat alone when your belly is full is bad manners.

Democracy is not a monopoly of those who wield the biggest stick. A slave-driver cannot continue leading the people forever because the slaves will rebel and fight back, and in the end they will be victorious. After all, they have nothing to lose except their chains of bondage. And they have their dignity to gain.

Zimbabwe is in a state of anarchy. The laws that our own parliament has made have been thrown into the rubbish bin. The ruling party thinks anarchy can be cherished for political expediency. No ruling party can just ignore the laws of the land and survive. No country will accept tyranny, even if they have to endure it for a while. Democracy will prevail, people will speak out.

✤ Rural Teachers, Rural Buses ✤ and Violent ZANU(PF)

I love buses, especially rural ones. I would prefer the train if I had a choice, but, unfortunately, it does not go everywhere. When I was a little boy, I had the pleasure of riding in a train in the company of itinerant musicians such as John White, Ngwaru Mapundu, and a man called Mhungu. They used to travel by train playing music for which they made the passengers pay sixpence, and a tickey for children. Everyone in the coach enjoyed the music as it spilled over us. And everyone was happy!

Now, I love rural buses and rural teachers. They have something in common – buses and teachers. You see a teacher leaving a bus, with a bag in his hands, out there in the countryside.

'Teacher, how are you? Have you come from the city again?'

'Yes, Baba, I am coming from the city. How is your health? I remember your grandson was not feeling well last week,' responds the teacher.

'Oh, children will always be children. It was just a flu or something else,' the old man smiles. 'I saw you leaving the bus and wondered if you had brought me an old newspaper so I can roll my cigarette.'

The teacher takes out his new newspaper. He selects a page that is full of nothing and gives it to the old man, who takes his pouch of 'Shamrock' and rolls his first cigarette in three days.

'Thank you Teacher. In these parts, the temptation to use the grandchild's exercise book for rolling cigarettes is quite high,' the old man says, licking the newly rolled cigarette before asking Teacher for 'fire' to light it. And when the latter brings out a lighter, the old man gives him a quizzical smile. 'So, you go to the city to find all these new-fangled things? It is nice to send children to school. That is why I restrained myself from using a page from the child's book for my cigarette. I want him to be like you,' the old man smiles and vanishes into the fields.

Teacher came by bus from the city. Among the citizens of the village, he is the only one who earns a regular monthly income. We are not ignoring the agricultural officer, the nurse and the local shop owner. But now we talk of the Teacher because of the crowds that he commands.

The Teacher goes to town at the end of every month to cash his pay cheque. He takes the local bus although it will take him the whole day to reach his destination, and another whole day to return. Even if he is late, the Head Teacher forgives him. Otherwise what is the Head Teacher without teachers to head? Teacher takes ideas from the village, mixes them with ideas from the city, and brings back a goulash to the village where he works.

The road has been graded. It is a road. The bus travels to town along the road, carrying Teacher. But when Teacher returns from the city, he brings new alcoholic drinks like brandy, gin, probably even whisky if the other foreign-based uncle happens to have been in the city. The locals are worn out drinking the local seven-day brew, Chibuku. Teacher drinks *hwemabhotoro*, bottled beer.

But Teacher also brings books for the children and a few for himself so that he can sharpen his brains, which have a high risk of rusting while he is far away from the city. Out there in Dande, to talk of a library is to talk of madness. Teacher knows it.

Alongside the books, Teacher brings newspapers, many of them, old and new, which his Uncle Peter has been keeping for him in the city. Uncle Peter knows that Teacher needs old newspapers for use as toilet paper. But teacher also needs new newspapers for sharpening his ideas on day-to-day events.

You know what a road does? It carries people and ideas. That is why African politicians do not trust roads. They are a dangerous piece of development. The politicians do not like buses either. Roads bring Teacher to the countryside, which would be silent if Teacher had not come there with his ideas about a new political party that likely to take over from the old ruling party.

For a desperate politician, the bus is as dangerous as the Teacher who is as dangerous as the road which carries both of them.

Did I say a bus? Yes, you see, these days the bus does not only bring Teacher in the flesh. It brings music. The bus owner is some mischievous guy who paints all sorts of things on his bus. *'Ndoinda Dande'. 'Bvuma Wasakara'. 'Mhofu Ndizvo'. 'Mamvemve'.*[4] 'Disaster.' And so forth. To the point of painting all sorts of things on the metal body.

Someone had painted *'Ndizvo'* on the metal body, so the villagers wondered what *'Ndizvo'* was all about. A villager walks two kilometres to the Teacher to find out what this *'Ndizvo'* is all about. After Teacher has explained, the elder says, with a gentle nod, 'It is good to travel, my child,' before walking away. *'Kufamba huona'* (To travel is to see), the old man thinks.

Rural buses, teachers and the ruling party. These three are a recipe for political violence. The bus conductor is armed with the music in his bus. The teacher is armed with ideas in a place where ideas are welcome. The ruling party is armed with real guns. Shoot to kill. And do not even bother to ask questions later. *'Mateacher neZANU(PF) zvakasonana veduwe-e'* (Teachers and ZANU(PF) do not see eye to eye, my friends), I said at the time of the June 2000 parliamentary elections. And I can say the same for the Bikita West madness as well as the presidential election madness.

Teacher, look out!

You see the rural teacher is respected in his community. He earns money, and everyone knows it. Every desperate villager goes to him, either to borrow a bicycle or to ask for some money to send the little child to school so the boy can be like Teacher. If it so happens that Teacher has a car, his car becomes communal property for the villagers to take the sick and the old to the nearest clinic. If the chief runs short of ideas, Teacher is there to give some learned answers on matters of local government and politics.

Teacher. That is why Teacher is the first target of violence by ZANU(PF). The ruling party wishes it could post a few youths at every growth point, with tins of paint so that they repaint all those buses with horrible slogans deriding the new political parties. But they cannot afford it. They send youths with boxes of matches to burn the buses that bring such wrong ideas to the villagers. They also wish roads had not been constructed to some parts of the country so that everyone would stay where they have always been, without having Teacher travelling to and from the city, conveying dangerous new ideas.

Rural roads carry rural buses that carry rural people. And people carry ideas, strange ones at that. No ruling party in Africa likes these three things, especially if Teacher is involved. Since Teacher brings new and old newspapers to the villagers and, when necessary, reads to them, he is the first target of political violence.

At election time, the bus has to be stopped so that Teacher can be subdued to silence. Schools have to be closed so that Teacher is barred from exposing his new ideas that he has brought from the city of violence.

I hear that in Bikita West, the ruling party activists have occupied a school, and Teacher is confused. He does not know what to do, now there is some guy wearing a hat which looks like a bird's nest in the school yard.

The bridge does not have to be repaired for the time being so that Teacher with his strange ideas, strange clothes and strange new drinks can be kept away from 'innocent villagers'. Teacher, please do be careful!

You see, when the ruling party introduces new regulations against civil servants participating in politics, it is Teacher who is the target. Since Teacher is listened to all the time, even if he might not have all the relevant data, he is trusted in the villages.

Anyway, Teacher, please be careful. Presidential elections are not long away. You will be raped, beaten up, kidnapped, insulted, undressed and decapitated. Please be careful. If you run away from the countryside, our children will die illiterate like some politicians who went to school but have started hating Teacher. If you hate Teacher, you hate new ideas. And if you hate new ideas, you hate the road and the rural bus.

Shades of Power: Colonial and Post-Colonial Experiences of a Writer.

I was born into a large African family, and by large I mean large. That was during the Federation of Rhodesia and Nyasaland, when there were virtually no borders between the three countries that comprised this union. It was a time of migration. My father wanted to go to Zambia where land was plentiful, but he had a large family and he was a chief. Chiefs don't just pack their bags and leave.

Each one of his several wives was our mother. My father did not permit us to call the older wives *maiguru* (elder mother), or the younger ones *mainini* (young mother). According to him each one of them was to be called mother. That was not the normal custom but when my father made up his mind about something, that was that. And he did not hesitate to use the whip on any one of us. You might say he was some type of Okonkwo,[5] but his regime functioned. We grew up happily and sometimes sadly, in the grip of his authority and control.

He provided my first experience of power and influence. For there were men and women who tried to influence my father to change the obvious results of a court case. Afterwards, he would tell us, 'That man is foolish, how can I keep my reputation if I rule in his favour in a case as obvious as this?' During the trial, he would do the least talking while his assistants heard the man out. At the end of the day, my father would tell him that he had not argued his case properly.

Several wives? What about the Christianity that the Swedish missionaries brought to our part of the world? Well, when my father discovered they would have no truck with a polygamous union, he ignored them. He was a chief, and no one could tell him to abandon the life of his ancestors. But he was passionately concerned that we should receive the white man's education. In this sense, he was like Ezeulu in Achebe's *Arrow of God*. It irritated him to have to go to the District Commissioner's office to be dictated to by other people's sons. He wanted his own sons to have the education to be the small policemen, administrators, and so on.

Another nuance of power. My father never imagined that Africans would displace the white man in the larger offices of power, such as that of the District Commissioner. I still recall some of his descriptions of the DC having tea, writing documents, retrieving files. Tea became a symbol of power, alongside the pen, which the DC so casually inserted behind his ear. That was power. The power of tea and pen, the power of office, and the power of language and translators who always seemed determined to humiliate you. These were the basis of our encounters with power in those years of colonial solitude and doubt. It was taken for granted that power belonged to the white man. No one doubted it.

The other vehicle of power that I encountered early on was the school inspector. I still remember how Mr Nordish, the missionary inspector of schools, was the terror of every teacher in the area. He would sneak into a school after abandoning his Landrover a safe distance from the school. If he found a teacher seated twiddling his thumbs or beating up a child, he would physically rebuke the teacher in front of us, the children. And we celebrated to see a bully meeting his match.

I started learning English when I was over twelve years old. Before then, we had our own nursery schools where we played *mahumbwe*, (playing house) and imitated our parents in their roles. Folk tales formed part of our literary diet, especially once the harvest was in. We herded cattle and learnt the laws of the jungle, naming the birds and lizards before killing them for both fun and food. But the most important lesson for me during that time was that we learnt that men, dogs, and cattle were taxed. Women were not taxed. They remained minors till death.

Colonial taxes made my father determined that he would only send boys to school so they could become administrators or clerks who would be able to pay their own taxes. Girls were only destined to remain in school until they could read and write. Then they were ripe for marriage. So, at least, my father argued. They were able, he said, to read the letters from their potential suitors without having to go through the humiliation of asking someone to read such secrets for them. 'Read the letter to me Marita,' someone says to the young woman in *Bones*.[6] The burden of illiteracy! The inability to read one's own destiny. By illiteracy, I don't mean only or even essentially not being able to read, I mean not being able to identify where you are and how you want to proceed to the next destination.

In time, my father decided that the family should move to the north of the country, in search of fertile land. We moved in the early 1960s to new lands, new soils, new landscapes, and a new sky wielding a new sun. As teenagers, we had to learn afresh the names of the new birds we encountered, new trees, new grasses and new people. We were in exile, and some of you who have read my novel *Shadows* will recall the exile that I lived. For once, we could not play in the moonlight because the forests of those lands were infested with lions and other hungry beasts. And worse still, the owners of these lands had been forcibly moved somewhere else.

But in both school and college, the expressions 'African writer' or 'African literature' were not part of the vocabulary of my literary experience. It was only with the insistence of one Toby Moyana that we began to read works by African writers during the last years of college. *Things Fall Apart, Song of Lawino, The Beautyful Ones Are Not Yet Born, Arrow of God*[7] . The floodgates opened in terms of individual and collective identity. I discovered that we were Africans and there were other Africans out there who were busy waiting for us to join the train of history, to make our own destiny.

Again, new metaphors of a new experience imposed on us by the colonial period.

The liberation war came and found us. Alienation took many forms since all the fighting factions and groups appeared, each selecting their own sell-outs to kill at will. By that time I was already working, teaching children good English.

Most people wonder why the liberation war is so important as a literary event during the de-colonisation process. The war gave us a new experience and we had to search for a new language with which to name things. The soil as our place became a real possibility, and the sky became, for the first time, our communal geographical and spiritual space, one which we could own for ourselves and our children. In other words, the liberation war was a re-shaping of our destiny. Our stars became different. Our stories, our history, held new potential. We could re-create them, to tell ourselves our own truth, our own lies, like everyone else. In other words, the liberation war was the birth of a new conscience.

It is important to note that before 1980, few if any major works were published by black Zimbabweans inside the country, although the Literature Bureau and Mambo Press made valiant efforts. Then at independence in 1980, literature suddenly blossomed. The poetry anthology, *And Now the Poets Speak*[8], was a massive celebration of poetry in English, by blacks. Good or bad English, it did not matter. The language had been harnessed for our own use. It was ours to use as we wanted. It was not a foreign language any more. In that anthology, politicians, prisoners, priests, prophets, farmers, and midwives were transformed into poets. The world had opened, and the sky was no longer the limit.

For academics, that 'transformation' is one they call a 'transition'. It lasted a few years. But all too soon, the black politicians were among us, wielding their own shades of power. The songs of praise waned as they criss-crossed the land in Mercs so dark inside that you could hardly see them. They waved at us as we walked the pavements, calling us their people, *povo*,[9] which the humourists quickly told stood for 'people of varied opinions'.

New images invade the writer. Shimmer Chinodya spanned the period from the 1960s to the 1980s in *Dew in the Morning*. Should we call such literature post-colonial or colonial, or neither? One of my novels, *Ancestors* spans a period of nearly one hundred and fifty years. The creation of the work began in 1988, but conception had begun many years before our independence in 1980. One always wants to ask: is the colonial or post-colonial a historical or psychological space? It is for the academics to answer. But the writer writes, creates, and pours out the images and metaphors given to him by a combination of history, feeling, and imagination.

In this whole act, a historian is one who thinks and analyses history, and a writer or artist is one who feels history, be it colonial or post-colonial. I always tell people that if they want to know about the history of a country, do not go to the history books, go to the fiction. Fiction is not fiction. It is the substance and heartbeat of a people's life, here, now, and in the past.

In a confused world like ours, which some investors have decided to call the global village, categories only serve to assist the critic to analyse in a more or less sensible way. In a village, where I grew up, everyone knew everyone. But in this new global village, no one knows anyone except through technology to which the villager has no access.

As it is, categories are only models created for the joy of those whose job it is to categorise.

Streams of Power

The other day I was sitting, not minding anybody's business, when I read some new political nonsense – a new crop of politicians who have been offered ministerial posts without a shred of the right kind of experience.

You see there are streams of power in which you must swim before you arrive. In Shona we say, '*hove dzinouya nemuronga*' (fish follow the stream). Imagine that your father and mother had never run a tuckshop, and you too had never run a tuckshop, but one day you wake up to find that you have been appointed the general manager of a whole chain of supermarkets. The mess that is likely to emerge from your 'promotion' is really immense.

Free goodies are likely to be given away to friends instead of being sold. Workers are likely to be abused instead of motivated and properly rewarded. Relatives are likely to be promoted to managerial positions. Authority, power, needs some kind of background and training. There are many that have come from humble beginnings and worked their way to the top, learning and gaining experience as they go.

It is a disaster if a man or woman who has never been a prefect, or the head of department in a school, is suddenly made the head teacher. What a frightening event! The person has not swum the stream of experience that would qualify him or her to head a school.

What will happen? Teachers are likely to be transferred without the proper forms being completed. Students will be beaten up in the name of discipline. Books will go missing and find their way to the headmaster's children. School fees paid will be regarded as someone's own pocket money. At the very least you should be a senior teacher before you can qualify to become the school head. Short cuts breed arrogance and contempt.

Let us look at the game of political power. If a man has never been elected to public office, he should never be given political power. And when it happens as it has in Zimbabwe, there is a disaster.

Individuals suddenly elevated to high office seem to realise the dangers of power. 'Power tends to corrupt and absolute power corrupts absolutely.' Power shrinks the human conscience until it often disappears.

Take, for example, a certain university professor, who is suddenly given responsibility for several government ministries. He takes it upon himself to speak for others. He takes it upon himself to decide who is and who is not a patriot. He gives himself responsibility for defining patriotism. And so it goes, he is the authority on everything: history, foreign affairs, broadcasting, journalism, development, agriculture, etcetera.

Such is power that is assumed without the necessary experience and humility. Power properly understood and administered requires dialogue and communication: to listen, to hear, to have humility. Pomposity is a bad ingredient of power.

Now the *povo*, the people of varied opinions, begin to wonder if he has elected himself Prime Minister? Mr first-above-all, Prime Minister Professor Doctor So-and-so, MA, PhD etc! Of all things, the most important aspect of power is humility. If you are not humble, if you do not see that your job is to serve the people, the chances are that you will become a tyrant. You will lose your conscience.

 60

Surprisingly, some of our ministers, ones who are only too happy to talk about and on behalf of 'the people, the *povo*, the masses' don't even have a constituency. They have not even been elected. Such men are often dangerous. They taste a little power and it runs to their heads. One has to understand power; one has to know how to dress it, how to share it with others, and how to use it to achieve positive results for the community or the nation. What a shame if a minister or head of state if feared by his or her citizens. Public office requires a commitment to those on whose behalf you are exercising your mandate.

The Ibo people of Nigeria say: 'He who gave you power is also the same one who did not give it to me.' In other words you may have power today, but not tomorrow. *Usavhaira nemasimba*. (Don't get carried away by your power.)

Funnily enough, when you are in a position of authority, you do not own the people. The people own you. Never mind that they did not receive the same education. No, but they went to the real school: the school of life. Those villagers whom some leaders have dared to call '*my* people' will tell you: '*Chinobhururuka chinomhara*,' (That which flies will eventually perch). You can fly today with wings of power, but one day they will be clipped.

Anyone who rises to power has a duty to reflect on it. Without reflection, power becomes an instrument that will lead to decay. And it is shocking when a human conscience decays in broad daylight.

The Fear of Ideas

These days it is hard to wake up. Hard because what you see as you wake up makes you feel that you are not in the same country you once believed in, and still live in. Violence and lawlessness are parading as governance in our once lovely country. The flowers, trees, birds and rivers of our land, which once nourished our imagination, have all been taken over by those without any appreciation of this beauty, this nourishment.

A policeman is guarding newspapers so that vendors can sell them. A vendor is watching out for militants who might destroy them. *Nhai veduwe e!* (Oh goodness me! what is happening?) The fall of the kingdom begins with the death of ideas. This can be done by killing the people who produce the ideas and destroying the machinery by which they can be disseminated to the public.

Sadly, our own government has started killing ideas and trying to silence those who produce them. If, however, you are a man of peace, you might quarrel with the idea, but you will not kill the person who holds it, otherwise there will be no one to argue with. What is a man without argument and debate? What is a woman without a discussion at the water well? Totalitarian regimes begin by killing ideas and then they kill the producers of those ideas.

A bad government specialises in silencing its own thinkers and the means by which ideas are disseminated. What is a printing press? A machine that William Caxton first invented in 1476, so that ideas could be circulated far and wide. Once a government begins to condemn and silence any ideas not their own, people must know that they have a problem on their hands: a big problem called dictatorship.

At worst, a dictatorship will burn books and bomb printing machines; burn bookshops and imprison the writers, publishers and editors. At worst, a dictatorship will hire wives to spy on their husbands, and husbands to spy on their wives. At worst, a dictatorship demands the face of their dear leader on every wall in the country. And so on.

Our country is in a state of fear. Those who grew up under Smith's state of emergency now recognise that the real state of emergency has only just begun. It was one thing to be oppressed by a colonial regime. It is another to be oppressed by your own people. They are the ones who should have our welfare at heart, so when they oppress us, we know we are living through a time of anguish.

The other day I was talking to an old man. He was insistent that his sons and daughters should not go beyond O-level. 'Why?' I asked. 'Look at our current leaders with their university degrees,' he said, 'Have they been able to do anything for anyone except themselves?' Zimbabwe is no longer run by our elected representatives, instead it is run by appointed hooligans and thugs. They have no public mandate; they do not know what the concept means. They have no sense of accountability. The report to no citizen, no responsible constituency.

It is high time the people of Zimbabwe said 'enough' and chose not to be ruled by those who have no respect for them. We have our own Goebbels[10] and we don't want any such person. The time of thinking in arbitrary two-year (so-called) development terms is over. We must think ahead to the next fifty or five hundred years. My only appeal to the President of the Republic is: Please return this country to sanity, and the rule of law and human conscience.

Only God and truth can help us now. Those who deny the truth now, deny the reality, will have to face it one day. Now we may feel reduced to a shadow of what we can be and were. Our flower has withered in the garden of hope.

⅋ The Two Faces of Africa ⅋

I and a few other writers were once stranded in the desert: no water, no diesel for the four-wheel drive, no food. We were near a Tuareg village but we had no language to explain our plight. The villagers saw us and left us alone, suspicious of the strangers sitting in the midst of their sand-dunes and camels.

After marvelling at how far we were away from all we knew, we decided that I, as group leader, and a West African writer should go to meet the villagers, though we could not utter a word of their language and they spoke neither French nor English, nor even Bambara or Fulani. But we had to negotiate some food.

This did not take long. Soon we had bought a goat. The villagers then volunteered to kill and skin it for us, and they even provided us with firewood in the midst of sand dunes. By the end of the afternoon, one villager and his family had decided that I was their son. I was invited to their home and taken on a tour. They showed me their architecture and how it enables them to withstand the burning desert heat.

For sure, I was their son. Without speaking a word of the same language, we understood each other. We used the timeless language of signs. And the jokes came and went, right into the middle of the night. One face of Africa, so full of love and beauty, ready to celebrate life wherever it is found. Africa without borders, without hindrances.

We can say the same for any part of Zimbabwe or Zambia or Nigeria. People are always ready to welcome strangers. In fact, it is the duty of every community to ensure that a stranger is well cared for. After all, the Shona say, *'muenzi haapedzi dura'* (A stranger passing by will never exhaust your granary). This face of Africa enriches life and human experience.

Now to the other face of Africa, the ugly one.

A ruler is elected to power. And the first item on his agenda is to buy as many guns and bullets as possible. Handcuffs, baton sticks, armoured cars, the latest fighter jets, tear-gas, and so on, just in case he has to use them against his own unarmed people. They wonder who the enemy is and when a war is about to commence.

If villagers dare to protest to the leader about their poor conditions, their need for land, fertilisers, health care, education, they are confronted by heavily-armed men and women who have instructions to shoot. Their birthright, the love shown to me by the people in the desert, is not there. All the ugliness of a people is concentrated in one person. But those employed to do the president's bidding are not about to lose their jobs. They will shoot to kill. But that same political leader was no doubt taught lessons in human compassion and love in his village.

Look at the madness engulfing Zimbabwe at the moment. Our rulers cherish the violence. They want it for the sake of retaining power. I wonder what would happen if someone dared to ask: 'Did your mother tell you to kill other human beings so that you could remain in power?' I am sure the answer to that question would be death. The questioner would not live to give us an answer.

The ugly face of Africa seems to surface at very inconvenient times. With power in their hands and hearts, Africans soon forget to smile in their usual enriching way. Political leaders soon think they are demi-gods with the power to dish out dollops of heaven or hell to the citizenry. Flatterers and praise-singers receive small portions of heaven. Honest citizens who are openly critical of the excesses of power are soon reminded of hell.

It was the Nigerian novelist, Chinua Achebe, who said the problem with Africa is lack of a visionary leadership. He was right. A political leader who builds a million-dollar mansion just a few kilometres from very poor communal lands does not have vision. A leader with imagination and vision would be challenged by the contrast between extreme poverty and extreme wealth.

The other day, one of our very own ministers paid for a very expensive dinner. When he was asked why it was that he could spend so much money on so few, with no sense of irony he translated the expense into US dollars and then said it was cheap. But who earns US dollars? The amount he spent in one night could have fed a whole school for a week.

Most of our politicians need to go to night school to learn a few basic things about good governance. The syllabus might contain a course on truthfulness and honesty; another on the basics of respecting public funds and using them for the public good; a course on the abuses of power; and one on the use of common sense.

Our politicians, especially those in the current ruling party, can brazenly lie and keep a straight face. They will say that politics is a game. How can you call politics a game? Only when African politicians play using the skulls of its citizens as footballs.

When people starve or drown after flooding, the politician will insist on 'jetting in' to the flooded areas, where they are happy to receive gifts. During the floods of 2000, I saw politicians accepting watermelons from people who no longer had homes. Instead of taking assistance to the benighted villagers, the politicians took what little they had away.

Of Africa's two faces, the ugly one seems to prevail over the beautiful one. Our leaders inflict so much pain and sorrow that one wonders what their parents taught them when they were growing up. Even those who go to church every Sunday seem only to go to be seen. Soon after the service, they will give new and brutal orders. They have no compunction about stealing public funds despite the sixth commandment: thou shall not steal. I have come to accept that most politicians are crooks. But while western politicians steal from rich coffers leaving something for the people, African politicians steal from coffers which they have almost emptied.

The burden of Africa is big. Without visionary leaders, we will have to beg from donors for a long time to come. The dream of an African Union will remain a pipedream. We cannot unite the continent when there is so much ugliness in each of our own countries. That respect for life that most poor, humble and cultured Africans possess is too soon forgotten by the rich and powerful.

ॐ The Violence of Gokwe ॐ

Many people must be wondering why there is so much political violence in Gokwe (or Gogwe, as villagers call it) which has been my home area since the early sixties. I know more about Gokwe than the place where I was born, just outside Zvishavane, and not far from Mberengwa.

First, Gokwe is the biggest district in the whole country, with a population of no less than a million and half. With just a handful of MPs to represent the district, the constituencies there are so large that not a single Member of Parliament in the area has managed to visit the whole of his or her constituency in five years. Some MPs don't even have the slightest idea where the boundaries of their constituency are.

Gokwe borders with Kwekwe, Gweru, Matebeleland North (Binga), Kadoma, Chinhoyi/Karoi, and to cross the district, never mind the bad roads, you will be at the wheel for a good day of hard driving. Gokwe is Korekore country, the belt of the ethnic group that stretches from Guruve to Binga, Kadoma to Binga. Gokwe is vast.

Another observation to be made about Gokwe is that it is probably the richest area in the whole country. It has gold, copper and one of the biggest coal mines in the whole of southern Africa. The majority of the people living in Gokwe migrated there from other parts of the country in search of farming land, and they do actually farm. They produce thousands of tonnes of cotton and maize. Despite this the district is one of the least developed in the country. In many places, there are no roads, no clinics, no schools. So the people of Gokwe are angry and rebellious because the Mugabe government has ignored them for twenty years. Given a clear and non-violent election, several million votes would go to the opposition.

Now, what has all this to do with the violence, you may ask. Well, sadly not one MP for Gokwe has ever stood up to denounce the violence. There is even a Minister of State who comes from Gokwe who must know full well about the death camps scattered throughout the district.

In the turbulent years, 1977-78, just before independence, Gokwe was a military goulash: one found Zanla and Zipra[11] forces, plus Rhodesian soldiers. They were all hunting each other down.

And, as usual, when two elephants fight, it is the grass that suffers. There were so many so-called 'sell-outs' it was unbelievable. People of Shona origin would sell-out their neighbours of Ndebele origin and *vice versa*; those who were tortured by the Rhodesian forces would sell-out both the Shona and the Ndebele.

On observing that the military situation was beyond them, the Rhodesians introduced the Selous Scouts as well as Abel Muzorewa's *dzakutsaku*,[12] fully armed, and Ndabaningi Sithole's militias. So, there were Rhodesians, *pfumo revanhu*,[13] *dzakutsaku*, and all sorts of other characters wielding various weapons. Each of these militias recruited local boys to join their sides, and they revenged on their neighbours for whatever real or imagined harassment had been inflicted upon them. You can imagine the killings, the murders, and the refugees who flocked to the cities – Kwe Kwe and Kadoma, in particular. My father and our whole family formed part of that exodus, abandoning cattle, tractors, maize, full granaries: everything.

At the time of the ceasefire, all the many armed militias in Gokwe could not be integrated into the national army. So, the Rhodesian soldiers decided on a solution. They called them all to assemble at Nembudzia centre, just outside the township, saying that the militias were going to be paid off and allowed home. Many armed youths assembled. The Rhodesian military knew they had taught these young people to kill and torture at will, so they decided to rid themselves of the problem by sending military planes to bomb the centre. Hundreds of youth were killed. They were all buried in mass graves dug by Caterpillars. All this happened at Nembudzia where the ruling party has now also established a murder and torture base.

After independence came the 'dissident' period and Gokwe was once again at the forefront of the violence. The new army of Prime Minister Mugabe went in to kill its own 'sell-outs', and the 'dissidents' did the same. It was another brutal period and not what Gokwe either needed or expected when it was trying to recover from the liberation war. Again my father became a refugee in Kadoma. Families were wrecked, farms destroyed, and hope as well. The ruling party now claims it is fighting to give people land but why then is there a murder and torture base at Nembudzia where opposition party members have been tortured, raped, and killed? Once again there are refugees in Kadoma, Kwe Kwe and Karoi. Gokwe, like Mutoko and parts of Guruve, are no-go areas for anyone who does not have a ruling party card. I do not have such a card, or any card for that matter, and so I am an exile from my own home. The area is sealed off with ZANU(PF) thugs and militias wielding guns and sticks, throwing stones, stopping buses, interrogating passengers, torturing whoever offends them.

The truth is that the violence in Gokwe has nothing to do with any so-called land redistribution. It is simply political violence based on the ruling party's strong belief in violence for political gain.

We know from our experience and common sense that when leaders take democracy away from the people, they are like birds whose wings have been severely clipped. But we also know that feathers grow again. You cannot trim a bird's wings forever. One day it will fly, and fly high.

✤ Two Ears and One Mouth ✤

Once upon a time there was a rich man in a village, so rich that everyone knew him and his dogs. You needed two days to count his cattle, and a whole afternoon to count his goats and sheep. The man was rich.

People had loved him when he was young and worked hard. But he had changed as he got older and richer. He did not talk to anyone politely any more. He only invited people to his house to give them instructions about what he wanted them to do. He did not think to ask them for their ideas.

One day, as he worked in his fields, driving his latest tractor, a little boy tried to wave him to stop so that he could deliver a small message.

'Little boy, what do you want? Can't you see that I am busy?' the man shouted at the boy, before lecturing him on the virtues of work and wealth. The boy stood there for a long time, looking mesmerised by the onslaught of words.

'But Sir, I only have a message to deliver,' the boy protested at last.

'I know. It is a message about sick aunts and ailing chickens,' the man guffawed.

'Okay young man, whoever sent you, I do not care. Tell them I am busy and I do not want to listen to stories about goat fights and such,' the rich man revved his new tractor with a flourish.

The more he worked, the more he neglected his neighbours, and the wealthier he became. His hair grew white, but he was rich enough to have hairdressers tint it black because he wanted to look young and attractive.

He thought it would improve his image even more if he hired a few singers, poets and historians to sing his praises. One poet called him the Son of God, another said, 'No, he is not the Son, but God himself.' The higher the tributes the praise-singers paid, the more they were rewarded. But many villagers wondered what had got into his head, a man whom they had brought up in the humble way of the ancestors. They could no longer understand him.

And if anyone dared to go to his homestead to caution him about his high-handed way, the rich man would not listen. Instead he talked and talked and talked until he was exhausted with talk. No visitor could get a word in edgeways. Because he had been respected in his youth, many people attempted to reach him, but he would not listen. Instead, again and again, he told everyone his life story about how hard-working he had been. Again and again he said he didn't have time for unimportant visitors. Sometimes he became very angry if people told him something he did not want to hear. He only liked the sound of his own voice.

So, life went on, and the man became more and more isolated. No one wanted or tried to talk to him anymore. If anyone dared, the man would not allow the adventurer to open his mouth, instead he would talk and talk and talk, as if his was the only voice on earth. But one day the rich man fell sick, and the small boy appeared again, this time with a written note.

'What do you want again, little brat?' the old man tried to shout at the boy, though his voice was hoarse.

'The message. The message. I brought you the message,' the boy spoke softly.

The rich man was not slow to summon one of his muscular guards to come and take the boy away and he was never seen again. But the muscular man had searched the pockets of little boy and removed the message before making him disappear. And he told the old man what he had done in case he decided to read it which, of course, one day he did.

'Two Ears, One Mouth,' the note read.

He was mystified. Was it an insult? Was it a warning? Was it in code? Did it contain a secret message? He pondered long on these words which to him were quite meaningless. Then one day as he was sitting in his garden alone overlooking his splendid fields, but still feeling rather lonely, he saw an old man pottering down the road. And because he was lonely and needed an audience, he called him over.

'Come here, old man,' he shouted. 'You are old, do you know the meaning of these strange words?'

The old man replied, 'I sent you this message a long time ago, by my grandson, who never came back. What is says is: "Two Ears and One Mouth." This means that you should listen for twice as long as you speak. If you speak for one hour, you should listen for two hours. That is why God gave us two ears and one mouth. If you had learned to do this a long time ago, maybe you wouldn't be so lonely.'

And the old man turned on his heel and walked away.

꩜ Violence without Conscience ꩜

I am sitting in some place. Faces arrive. They are looking for me. I wonder what is amiss. For them the world has turned upside down. They simply want help. Their car has been burnt. The house is in flames. I have to bear witness to it all. Their faces are swollen. They have nothing left except their hearts, except love, sorrow and a scattering of hope sprinkled with tears. There is nothing left in their hands.

We have leaders. Their job is to take care of the welfare of us all, including those who did not vote for them. It is the people's democratic right to vote for the person of their choice. Our leaders have to accept the results whatever they are. Unfortunately, the ruling party does not accept change, so now we have violence, brutality, abuse.

Difference is a great thing. Imagine that the gods had created us all the same. Thinking the same, walking, talking the same. Our ideas and the way we present them would be the same. Can you imagine a whole village of people nodding at the same time to the same idea expressed in the same way.

What a boring world it would be!

One of the qualities of a good leader is that he or she accepts that leadership is about managing the diversity of a society, a community, or even a family. There is nothing wrong with diversity, with difference.

Our country is going through a phase of unsurpassed barbarism in the form of violence experienced on our doorsteps every day. My thinking is that this brutality is simply based on greed and corruption. Greed for power, and corruption in the sense that every one of our leaders has been in place for so long, stealing, and abusing their privileges that they can think of no alternative world.

Let us acknowledge the old saying, 'what you plant is what you reap'. If you plant the tree of happiness, you harvest the fruits of that happiness. If you sow the seed of hatred, you will harvest the fruits of hatred. African leaders have forgotten how to sow the seeds of happiness. So, instead, they plant hatred in the hearts and minds of their citizenry. When the time to harvest comes, they have to run.

Brute force has never been a viable way of maintaining political power. Power can never be nurtured by violence. It can only be nourished on the basic human values of love, respect, care for the weak and consent.

The fact is that no matter how uninformed a person may be, they will at least know what they want to do with their lives. No one has the power to deny another the right to choose their destiny. In a situation of brute force, such as the one we have at the moment, the voter is supposed to be reduced to an unthinking creature, one that will open its mouth to be fed whatever nonsense the rulers want to impart.

Political campaigns should be times of political, social and cultural dialogue, not times of voter humiliation. Political dialogue means talking to the voters about what they want and what you can and cannot do. They have every right to ask questions about promises previously made and how you are going to put right what has gone wrong. They have every right to do that without finding a dead body in their homestead.

What amazes me about the ruling party of our country, is how they can imagine that if they break my arm I will wake up the following day, and use it to vote for them. After having buried my father, whom they have killed, how can they think that I will vote for them? I do not understand their logic.

I have always said that there should be no corpses on the road to the ballot box. Any political leader who depends on the number of people killed for their political survival cannot last.

Our political leaders attend church where they pray and appear to honour Christian values: Blessed are the meek for they shall see God: Love thy neighbour as thyself: Thou shalt not kill: Honour thy father and thy mother... But the ruling party is teaching young people to kill their own fathers and mothers. Why go to church? What hypocrisy!

There are so many things for which we should have reverence on earth: the natural world, the heavens, humanity. But it seems there are some who simply worship power. But power fades, it is not renewable by violence.

Political leaders who use violence have in effect told the nation that they lack legitimacy and credibility. They have run short of ideas. If we are in dire economic straits, the president should explain why, not with rhetoric but with reason. Zimbabwe is experiencing the recurrent African problem of a ruler without ideas, vision or compassion. Often the ruled are patient enough to wait and vote them out of office, so as to replace them with someone who has new energy, new vision.

May the foolishness of our leaders and all this violence pass from us. We do not deserve it. It is not a time in our history that we would wish to honour. Our destiny should not be measured in brutality, rape, crime and malice. It should, instead, be measured in dance, song, beauty and the celebration of life, not death.

🐝 Zimbabwe: A Writer's Personal 🐝 Reflections

I was born and grew up on a menu of folk tales, the spoken word, the tale as it is woven by the *sarungano*, the weaver of the tale. In an oral situation, words are free agents. They move and change shape according to the whims of the storyteller. And the teller herself is a manipulator of the psychology of others, a performer whose whole body forms part of the tale being told. Her movement, gestures, facial expressions, the raising and lowering of her voice, and even the backdrop of the dark night all form part of the story. That is why we saw ogres in our sleep, after a tale well told. The ogre was as real as the dark night of which we were part.

Audience participation came in many forms. In the first place, the storyteller did not impose herself on the hearers. It was the audience, small children, older children, youths who all came to demand, to request, to cajole her to tell one of the favourites from her repertoire.

I will insist on using the pronoun 'her' since traditionally, in Shona society, the storyteller was always a woman. The story was part of the nursing she did even before you were born. Men only told you stories about how your ethnic group defeated another and so on. Gentle stories for gentle minds were always told by women, elderly ones who understood the workings of malleable young minds.

Today, many people have gone to school to learn to read and write, to pin the word on the white page. Every time I sit on a local bus, there is a lot of noise. People talk. People crack jokes. People sing and, with the help of local brew, even dance on the bus. It is not like being on a bus in Europe where one wonders, because of the solemn silence, if everyone is going to a funeral. Zimbabweans, indeed most Africans, are talkers. Orality permeates their every pore. The pub, the workplace, the pavement, the church are all places for exchanging the spoken word. Silence is a threat to the existence of humans. Talk is vibrancy and a sign of life. The story will live on in memory.

As I grew up, the book became part of my life. But it always hindered the opportunity to chat, to gossip, to banter, to joke, to talk about the joys and sorrows of the night and day, and life's vicissitudes. But the book had to be read in order to pass school examinations, and to understand the Bible in missionary schools. But that was during the sixties and seventies. Even then I found that the mobile word, the one on which I had been brought up, was suppressed by the arrested word on the page. Sometimes the teacher insisted that you repeat a story in the same way you had told it before; so unlike my mother who told the same story every night, but told it differently according to the audience's taste and demand.

Zimbabweans want to talk, and they insist on doing so. Reading is a lonely exercise, just like writing. Zimbabwe is a nation of talkers. The new illiterates are the graduates with university degrees who only read books when they were at the university, and then only the ones they had to read. As soon as they had written their final examinations, they sold all their books at a knock-down price. Farewell to reading.

If Zimbabweans happen to read, they prefer to borrow the book rather than buy it. Why buy if I can borrow? The European book is meant for the shelf. The African book is meant for circulation. When I sell ten thousand copies of one of my titles in Europe, I know it means about five thousand readers. If I sell the same number of books in Africa, I know it means at least fifty thousand readers: the book circulates until it falls apart. In Europe, the book is arrested on the bookshelf.

I have always thought of reading as pleasurable, but it can also be lonely since it is the space in which the writer can invade and subvert the conscience of the reader in their private space.

Zimbabwe is enduring an economic crisis. People find it hard to buy basic essentials. What right have I to encourage people to buy books when they are starving? The politics of the belly is more demanding than the politics of knowledge, the politics of conscience. It is a matter of choice, and in this case, forced choice: the book versus the food basket.

A book is a slice of life. Not many people want slices. They want the whole loaf. And a book in Zimbabwe is an occasional slice. And just to show how reading is rated in my country: whenever I go to the bank and ask for a loan, the question is: where do you work, and what is your salary, with proof of a pay slip. If I say I am a writer, they say, 'Sorry sir, you do not have a regular income.' That is mistrust of the book.

As a writer, I have developed certain principles, from experience. If I go to a new country, I do not want to read its history from history books. I want to know who the country's important writers are. *The Violent Land*, by Jorge Amado, gave me more history of Brazil than I would ever get from history texts. The true history of Zimbabwe is found in the heartbeat of Zimbabwe's writers.

The land, for example, which is now being used as an election campaign gimmick, was written about many years ago by Charles Mungoshi in his great novel, *Waiting for The Rain*. Politicians do not read. So they have suddenly invented land grabs for the sake of power, without being able to grasp the proper spiritual and moral meaning of the soil, the land in which the ancestors reside.

On many occasions, I have argued for a national cultural and book policy. For me, a book policy ensures that there is no book hunger among children in school and those who have left school. Libraries in the townships and other places must be provided with books bought for the readers by the state. But whenever will we have anything like that? Suppose the state made it a rule that to remove book hunger, the Ministry of Education would buy ten thousand copies of every new book published locally by a local writer, to give to schools. Every school library would be full of books by local writers, giving children an initial taste of the world through the literature of the land. For it is in those works that the children will discover what their geographical, psychological and emotional landscape is about in order later to appreciate the landscapes of others, in other lands.

As for me, a book is a small shrine onto which I gently deposit a bunch of flowers described in words.

'A book, Oh, what a universe, it forms, informs and transforms.'

Endnotes

1   The Abuja Agreement resulted out of a meeting between Zimbabwe and representatives of the Australian, Canadian, Kenyan, Jamaican, Nigerian and South African governments, in September 2001. At the meeting chaired by President Obasanjo, Zimbabwe undertook to stop new farm occupations, delist farms that did not meet the criteria for resettlement, restore the rule of law and put an end to the violence in the country. Once these commitments were met, The United Kingdom agreed to release funds for land reform and resettlement.

2   College Press, Harare, 1999

3   Movement for Democratic Change

4   Bus slogans are often full of innuendo and allusion: 'Going to Dande', 'Accept that you are worn out', The eland totem is okay', 'Tattered clothes'.

5   The main character in *Things Fall Apart* by Chinua Achebe.

6   *Bones* by Chenjerai Hove. First published by Baobab Books, Harare in 1988.

7   Novels by respectively: Chinua Achebe, Okot p'Bitek, Ayi Kwei Armah, Chinua Achebe.

8   Mambo Press, Gweru, 1986

9   Portuguese terms for 'the people' used during the liberation war, and sometimes afterwards with a suggestion of superiority.

10   Joseph Geobbels (1807-1945) headed Hitler's Ministry of Enlightenment and Public Propaganda. His gift for mob oratory and his hatred of the Jews made him a powerful exponent of Nazism.

11   Zimbabwe African National Liberation Army and Zimbabwe African People's Revolutionary Army, the armed wings of ZANU and ZAPU.

[12] *dzakutsaku*: literally 'many' or 'multitude'. Used in a prophetic sense by the United African National Congress supporters to mean that it was 'the party for everyone', and with condescension by people who did not belong to the UANC to suggest people with no political direction.

[13] 'Spear of the people'.